EASTERGATE MEMORIES

compiled from old photographs

by

EASTERGATE LOCAL HISTORY GROUP

published by

EASTERGATE PARISH COUNCIL
1994

Tucked away in a quiet corner of West Sussex on the fertile coastal plain, Eastergate Village retains its rural peace. The village centre has changed little in hundred of years. The Norman church in the farmyard, the granary on its steddles, the gracious farmhouse and the barn have stood there since before the time of Elizabeth 1.

The modern age has encroached upon the northern and eastern sectors of the parish. It is serviced by two roads, Fontwell Avenue and Barnham Road, and a railway station. The newer houses have been built along the roads. The following photographs capture a more leisurely age when cars were a rarity.

Near the Manor Farmhouse and its seventeenth century granary can be seen the Parish Church of Eastergate which is dedicated to St George. It is mainly Norman with some evidence, still visible, of the church of the Domesday Book.

There are several interesting features which include the Roman bricks in the outer wall on the south side of the Chancel; the fourteenth century glass depicting the arms of Fitzalan quartered with those of de Warenne; and the sixteenth century west window built with the bequest left by Richard Bromer in his will dated 1534.

It is interesting to note in the photograph of the wedding of Miss E B Collins to Mr R W Troop in 1907 that the old vestry of the church can be seen and not the present one. The bride was the daughter of William Collins of Flint House. He was a church warden and a parish councillor. The groom came from Church Farm, Aldingbourne and his father was church warden of that parish church.

Eastergate Rectory, which ceased to be an ecclesiastical property when it was sold in 1976, is now two private residences.

The Victorian house was built in two stages. The Reverend E C Hutchinson, in 1840, borrowed a sum of £720 to build a portion of the rectory. In 1883, a further £1,000 was borrowed to complete the house.

The four and a half acres of ground presented problems to at least one incumbent's wife, who, in 1953 : -

> 'managed to get the 'south waste' down flat for the Garden Fete, and Marquees and stalls were placed on it, but it was still very rough and the task of keeping it under control was beyond me.'*

* Eastergate Church Records

The Wilkes Head became an Inn in 1803, six years after the death of the man whose name it is associated with - John Wilkes. He was an eighteenth century political reformer who championed the cause of the people. He attacked the Government and criticised the King's message to Parliament which resulted in his imprisonment in the Tower. Following his release, Chichester held a grand reception for him and the market cross was lit by forty-five pounds of candles. He was involved in many more political clashes and finally became Lord Mayor of London.

The building itself was constructed in 1746 and the cottages pictured with it in the photographs are the Old House and Brook House.

EASTERGATE.
1484

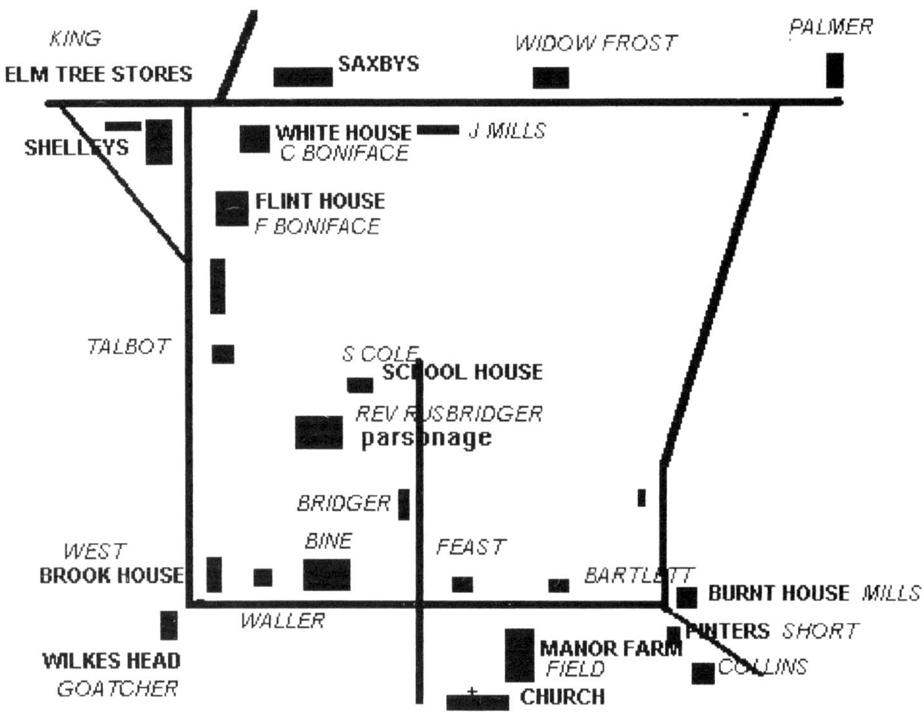

HOUSES AND THEIR OCCUPANTS IN EASTERGATE IN 1845. THE HOUSE PICTURED OPPOSITE IS THOUGHT TO BE THAT OF THE BRIDGER FAMILY IN SCHOOL LANE.

The lion statue on the War Memorial at Eastergate Square is a well known local monument which has recently been listed as of historical interest. It was dedicated in 1920 to commemorate those who fell in the Great War, 1914-1918. In the photograph it was surrounded by cannons which were donated for the Second World War effort.

The Lion is isolated on a busy traffic island today while some of the houses bordering roads in this area have been there for centuries, like the Thatched Cottage (dated 1623), Flint House and Malt House Cottages (seventeenth century), the White House, Shelley House and Elm Tree Stores (eighteenth century).

The photograph on page 17 shows that flooding in Eastergate is not a new occurrence.

THE SQUARE, EASTERGATE.

Flood at Eastergate 1915.

On the site which is now known as Daltons Food Centre was the saddlers shop which William Collins built for Mr Walling who lived in Slindon. He, originally, had a shop in the Nyton Road before moving to the new one in the Barnham Road. He rented the shop, which was a detached brick and corrugated iron building measuring 18 feet square, for £13.00 per annum. In it he sold harnesses and saddles as well as agricultural boots and shoes. The shop was sold in 1972.

In the photograph, taken outside the shop, are, left to right, Messrs Tim Lake, Bevis, Walling and Hann. The picture on the cover of this book shows the Thatched Cottage built in 1623 which is situated next to the saddlers shop and can still be seen next to Daltons Food Centre.

Further up the road towards Westergate, approximately 250 yards from Elm Tree Stores and the War Memorial, was the Smithy. It was owned by Mr Harry Gape who lived opposite in Forge Cottage. As well as looking after the needs of the local horses, it was also the first place in the area to sell petrol for the newer kind of horsepower.

Bognor Regis Water Company built the original Eastergate pumping station in 1895 at a cost of £10,000. The land was bought from William Collins for £100.

The Company's first well and tower were sited in London Road, Bognor, but as water consumption increased, so did the saline content. It was necessary to find a new source to the north.

Water was found in plenty at Eastergate on the second boring. The gush of water created a flood and the bore had to be capped quickly.

In 1913, when seasonal flooding occurred, a more permanent solution was found. A cast-iron plug was installed which could be raised or lowered according to the amount of water drawn. Neither this building nor the engines have survived.

Barnham Market began with auctions of livestock in 1882 and closed in 1949. In its heyday, it was a famous fat-stock market where 46,000 head of stock would be entered and sold each year.

Every Monday, cattle would be driven along local roads, or unloaded from trains, by drovers and butchers' boys. Farmers and buyers would ride to the market on horseback or in their dogcarts, floats or tub carts.

From 1910, the cattle were sold in the new shed. Sheep, pigs, calves and poultry were penned in rows out-of-doors. The corn exchange was in the market shop where garden produce, butter, cheese, eggs, second-hand furniture and tools were sold.

CATTLE MARKET EVERY MONDAY
85887 JV

The Eastergate/Barnham boundary follows the stream which has been responsible for many recent floods. In earlier times, it was crossed by Barnham Bridge. in the Quarter Sessions Order book of 1649 * it is recorded that it

'was lately in decay and ought to be repayred by the inhabitants of the sayd parishes at their equall charge....'

The nearby inn was called Barnham Bridge once. It was rebuilt in the early years of this century and is now the Barnham Hotel. On market days it was a popular meeting place for farmers, butchers and auctioneers and the venue for dinners after the famous fat stock shows.

* Quarter Sessions Order Book, Petworth, Michaelmas 1649
Sussex Record Society Volume 54

335.

From 1863, when Barnham Junction was opened, travel by train between London and Barnham was possible. In 1864, the Bognor line was opened. Gradually, the small agricultural community changed. Market gardeners could get their fresh produce to the London markets.

Because of the railway, the market was sited in Barnham. People who worked in the city or towns on the line, were able to commute each day.

The photograph on page 29 shows what is thought to be the opening of the Bognor Branch line on lst June, 1864. The station has changed much since then, including the opening of a new ticket office in 1929.

JUNCTION
BOGNOR

RNHAM JUNCTION
BOGNOR

Encouraged by the siting of Barnham Junction in the east of the parish, the area known as West Barnham slowly developed.

Sydney Marshall founded the West Barnham Estate Company in 1899 and bought land from the Ecclesiastical Commissioners. The Company built houses suitable for middle-class commuters along Barnham Road and Downview Road.

One of these houses was used by the firm Carter Patterson when they re-located to West Sussex on the out-break of World War II. Local people were employed. On nationalisation, in 1949, they became British Road Services and moved to Bournemouth taking some of their staff with them.

Since it was built in 1908, Eastergate Parish Hall has been a meeting place for the villagers. The stage has been the setting for countless productions. Clubs have met weekly to dance or play a variety of games. The Parish Council has held its meetings there. The side aisles were originally provided as rifle ranges for the Territorial Army.

Artists, including Byam Shaw, were commissioned to paint scenes from local history high on the walls and gallery. Poignant among these, are the names of men who were recruited at meetings in the hall to serve in World War 1 and who did not return.

The hall cost £2000 to build and A J Day of Fontwell house, Reverend W D Yoward of Eastergate and Captain Orr-Ewing of Aldingbourne shared the cost.

.. Sept. Commenced school again on Mona
last, after four weeks holiday.
The attendance this week has been
very poor, the average number
present being only half the number o
the books. Several are leasing, and
on Thursday many were away at
a Sunday School Treat at Yapston.
There was a holiday on Wednesday
and the children were taken to
Bognor by the 12.43 train, whence
after spending the afternoon by the
sea, and being regaled with Cake
and Lemonade, they returned about
half past five.

Eastergate has always been a lively place, many events being organised at the Village Hall, the Pub and the spacious sports ground. The Parish Council bought the four and a half acre sports ground from the auction of the late William Collins' estate, on the 3rd December 1941, for £725.

The photographs which follow illustrate a few of the events that occurred over the years and introduce a few local personalities.

Football 55 years ago

MR. PERCY EDWARDS, of 11 Central Drive, Bognor Regis (seated, second from left) has let us have this photograph taken in 1921 of EASTERGATE F.C. who, at the time, were playing in the Chichester District League.

Eastergate Football Team 1921

Wilkes Head customers

May Queen celebrations at Eastergate Sports Field

Fancy Dress Ball at Eastergate Parish Hall

Public Gathering at the War Memorial

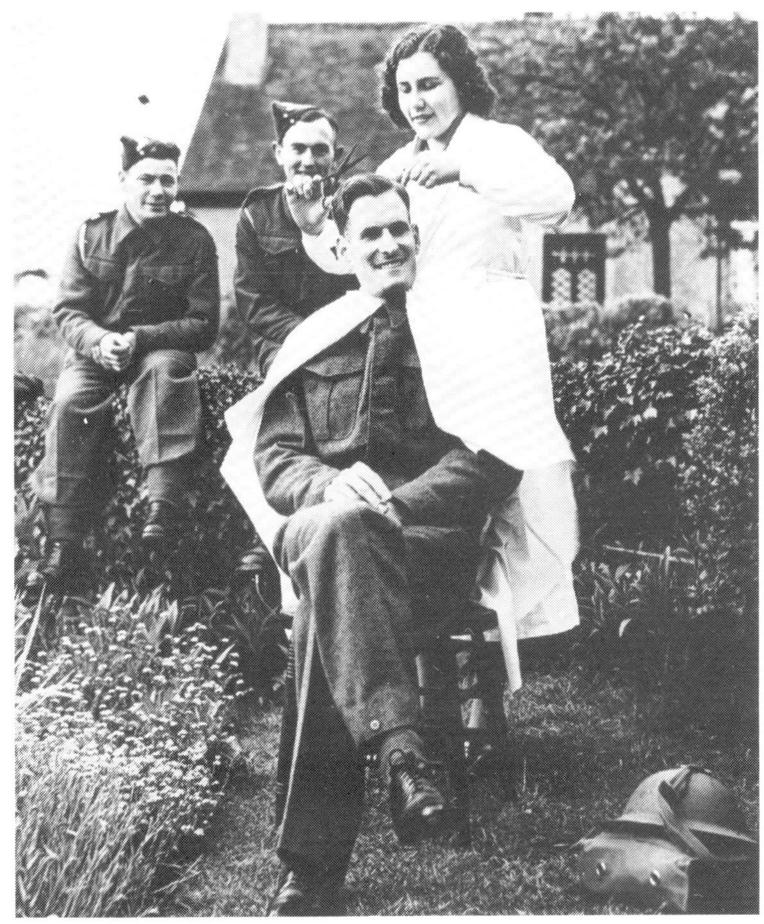

Connie Westbrook cutting soldiers' hair in her garden during war time. This photograph was used in a national newspaper.

1887

June 30th 1887 Queen Victoria's Golden Jubilee

Provisions to be supplied by William Collins for Eastergate celebrations

I agree to supply :-

Roast Beef and Boiled
Roast Mutton and
Boiled legs of Pork Bread Pickles etc. and Plum Puddings

for 200 men	2/6
working boys and women	1/6
200 children	6

Tea and Cake and Bread and Butter

Tables and stools and all necessary Crockery and Glass etc.

336 Men, Women & Boys and table clothes

200 children 130' long 24 wide

Arthur Northeast, sexton and verger of St George's church for many years lived at Malt House Cottages.

"Professor" Messam under the Elm Tree at Eastergate Square.

Acknowledgements

John Donabie, Sylvia Atkinson, Joan Barham, Gillian Bolan and Mary Botting would like to thank the following for their photographs and information:-

H Collins	S Hyland	B Watson
T Ford	J Jackson	D Wentworth
C Harding	A Timlick	C Westbrook

Bognor Regis Observer
Chichester Institute of Higher Education
Eastergate Church of England Primary School
Portsmouth Water plc
West Sussex County Record Office

The photographs were first displayed at an exhibition organised by Rosemary Collins on June 18th - 19th 1994 to celebrate the centenary of Parish Councils.

Technical details of copying old photographs -

Each print was copied using a Mamiya 645 medium format camera with an 80 mm standard lens. In addition two close up filters were used when close ups were required.

Illumination was by two Bowens Monobloc studio flash units placed at 45 degree angles from the subject.

Film was Ilford FP4 (120 roll film)

Processing was standard Aculux and printing was on glossy Multigrade paper